Jokes for Crescent City Kids

Jokes for Crescent City Kids

Michael Strecker

Illustrated by
Vernon Smith

PELICAN PUBLISHING COMPANY
GRETNA 2018

ISBN: 9781455624270
Ebook ISBN: 9781455624287

Printed in Canada
Published by Pelican Publishing Company, Inc.
1000 Burmaster Street, Gretna, Louisiana 70053
www.pelicanpub.com

To my wife, Jillian, and our Crescent City kids,
Stephen and Joseph

Why wouldn't the rich dessert go out with the sandwich?
It was a poor boy.

When will a New Orleans po'-boy shop serve a hero?
When Steve Gleason comes in.

What happened when the crawfish went to the party?

It ended up in hot water.

What would Caesar say to Brutus if he were Cajun?

"Étouffée, Brute?"

Where's the best place to open a barbershop in Louisiana?

Cut Off.

What does a Cajun baby get if he stubs his toe?
A beaux-beaux.

What famous singer could be Cajun?
Cher.

What should you do when you hear Cajun music?
Shake your Boutte.

What is a New Orleans girl's favorite beau?
    Gumbeau.

What happens if a Cajun forgets to make gumbo?
    He'll roux the day.

What's a good hairstyle for Mardi Gras?
A krewe cut.

Why did the New Orleans boy lose the National Spelling Bee?
The first word was "crew."

How do you know if people really love Mardi Gras?
They have a ball.

Why didn't the New Orleans actor get a part in the tragedy?
The second line made him dance.

What might you get if you are hit in the face with a Carnival throw?
Beady eyes.

Why did Rex shave on Mardi Gras?
He wanted to be a Smoothie King.

What ice-cream treat will you find at every Mardi Gras parade?
A float.

What would you call a dinosaur if he became king of Carnival?

T. Rex.

How can you help someone afford to have a parade?

Float them a loan.

How long does it take to form a Mardi Gras krewe?

Only a Momus.

Why was Rex's wife mad at him?
He was being a royal pain.

What do people say when the Comus king's float passes by?
"Who was that masked man?"

How do you tease a wealthy girl in a white dress?
With a debut-taunt.

What was the first thing the artist did when he was hired to create portraits of the Saints?

He Drew Brees.

How hard was it for the Saints to win the Super Bowl?

It was a Brees.

What do Saints receivers say to let Drew Brees know they're open?

"Throw me something, mister!"

What happened when the Who Dat ate too much?

He became Hubig.

Why did the Saints player have a knife and fork?
He needed to eat up the clock.

How long do Saints kickers have to practice?
Until they get it down to a tee.

What do you call it when the Saints beat a team 49 to 0?
Dome-a-nation.

What's the best champagne if the Saints win the Super Bowl?
Dome Pérignon.

Why did the Saints kicker study so hard?
He wanted to get extra points.

What sound does a New Orleans owl make?
"Who Dat!"

Why did LSU's football team hire an optometrist?
>   *To examine the eye of the tiger.*

What is a great university and a fun card game?
>   *UNO.*

How does a Martian say goodbye?
>   *He gives a Green Wave.*

Where can you get a great education and find great sales?
>   *Dillard's.*

What do you get if you cross a priest with a famous New Orleans musician?
Confessor Longhair.

What do you call Dave Malone in jail?
A busted Radiator.

If you wake up in a funk, what physician should you see?
Dr. John.

What saint loves loud music?
   St. Roch.

What do trumpet players do to stay in shape?
   Jazzercise.

What famous New Orleans musician lifted a lot of weights?
   Louis Armstrong.

What is the best slide in the world?
Slidell.

What does a Frenchman use to comb his hair?
La comb.

What does Al from the West Bank do when the ref makes a bad call?
Al jeers.

What do New Orleanians do when they get thirsty?
Bywater.

What's one snowman who can take the heat?
Mr. Bingle!

What would a Cajun call Santa Claus if he got a cold?
Papa No Well.

What did the clump of Spanish moss do on its birthday?
It had a Celebration in the Oaks.

What kind of Christmas tree do the pigeons in Jackson Square like?
A flocked one.

What do you call the ninth child of the Ward family?
The Ninth Ward.

What New Orleans TV station has programs about St. Patrick and cabbage?
The Irish Channel.

Where is a good place for a dollar to live?
Bucktown.

In what neighborhood does every home have blinds?
Venetian Isles.

What does Morris Bart wear to work every day?
A law suit.

Where are lawsuits decided by a couple of nuns?
The Court of Two Sisters.

What did the New Orleans astronaut tell his wife before the flight?
"I'll Michoud."

Where do New Orleans astronauts go to practice?
The Moon Walk.

What do they serve for dessert at Stennis Space Center?
Moon Pies.

Why did someone start the Moon Pie parade?
They had a pie-in-the-sky dream.

What do you call a sad fountain?
Fontainebleau.

What do you call a fountain owned by your father?
Popp's Fountain.

What do you call a fountain owned by a famous clarinet player?
Pete's Fountain.

What do you call Travers and Fletcher Mackel praying?

Holy Mackels.

What could you use to paddle your pirogue through storm waters?

A Margaret Orr.

Why did the New Orleans reporter bring a hatchet to the interview?

He wanted to axe *a question.*

What kind of chef makes a good lawyer?
  A sous chef.

Who's the most famous chef in New Orleans East?
  Chef Menteur.

What do you call a baby pig who makes everyone wait?
>   *A cochon delay.*

Why does everyone love Hogs for the Cause?
>   *It's not a boar.*

What's a great house for a duck hunter?
A shotgun.

What happened when the man hit the turducken with a slingshot?
He killed three birds with one stone.

What kind of underwear does Louisiana's state bird wear?
Pelican Briefs.

Where did the deer like to stay when it came to New Orleans?
Elk Place.

What are two good streets for writers to live on?
Read Boulevard and Magazine Street.

What would Edgar Allan Poe be if he moved to
New Orleans when he was a child?
Just another Poe boy.

What should you say to encourage a New
Orleans author?
"Yeah, you write."

What did the United States use to pay for the Louisiana Purchase?
French Quarters.

Why did the U.S. Mint open in New Orleans?
It made cents.

What is most difficult for a French Quarter street performer?
Juggling a career and family.

What do you call a French Quarter beagle who wins the Louisiana Lottery?
A Lucky Dog.

What do you call a mosquito at the Fair Grounds in late April and early May?

A Jazz Pest.

How did the man feel when he left the Seafood Festival?

Stuffed to the gills.

Why did the New Orleans Chihuahua need to go to the optometrist?
It had Popeyes!

What would happen if kittens joined the Krewe of Barkus?
It would reign cats and dogs.

What does a New Orleans dog do when it is thirsty?
It Barq's.

What Louisiana parish loves dogs?
St. Bernard.

What is a good fort for fish?
Fort Pike.

Where do leprechauns love to fish?
Irish Bayou.

Why did the man get fired from the Aquarium of the Americas?
He tried to plug in the electric eel.

Why was the man suspicious when someone offered him a lifetime pass to the Aquarium of the Americas?
It seemed fishy.

What did Ann do when the teacher told her to draw a historical figure?
Ann drew Jackson.

Why was the sketch of the Jackson Square carriage not very good?
It was horse drawn.

Why didn't anyone like Jackson?
He was a square.

How did the pigeons take over Jackson Square?
They staged a coo.

Where do oysters go to sunbathe?
  Shell Beach.

Are all shells the same shape?
  No, One Shell Square.

What is the richest bivalve?
Oyster Rockefeller.

What happened when Foster set his dessert on fire?
Everyone thought he was bananas.

Why did the New Orleans chicken cross the street?

To get to the neutral ground.

What do a median in New Orleans and the country of Switzerland have in common?

They are both neutral grounds.

Where can't you complain about a fly in your soup?
The Insectarium.

Where did the Crescent City insect learn to play soccer?
At the Fly.

What do you call a bunch of peas lined up
behind one another?
> *A pea row.*

Why was the steamboat so good at ping pong?
> *It had a big paddle.*

What's a crab that falls out of your net right before you put it in your bucket?
  A frustration crustacean.

What is the saddest crustacean?
  A blue crab.

How did the crab get to be boss?
  It clawed its way to the top.

Why was the ghost-tour guide upset when he made a mistake?

He knew it would come back to haunt him.

What's a good name for a Cajun ghost?

Boo-*dreaux.*

What could you say to scare someone named Ray?

"Bourré!"

What could you say to scare someone named Dan?

"Boudin!"

What do you call a werewolf from New Orleans?

A where y'at wolf.

What does a shrimper get if he makes a big catch?

Net profit.

What do shrimp wear when it rains?

Shrimp boots.

What do you get if you drop your shrimp on the beach?
Shrimp and grits.

What big festival sounds like the smallest festival in Louisiana?
The Shrimp Festival.

What kind of bread jumps out of the toaster by itself?

Bunny Bread.

What did the Leidenheimer and Reising families do when they came to New Orleans?

Made a lot of dough.

What is a New Orleans cow's favorite sandwich?

A moo-faletta.

What did the sandwich do before it left the restaurant?

It got dressed.

Why did the beignet want a phone?
  It needed to make a Morning Call.

What did the New Orleans bullfighter say?
  "Au lait!"

What kind of bird loves golf?
  An English tern.

What has wings, a magic wand, and white shrimp boots?
> *The Chalmette Fairy.*

What could you call a house in St. Bernard where everyone is always arguing?
> *The Chalmette Battlefield.*

Who works at the Chalmette Refinery?
> *101 Chalmatians.*

What did the Mississippi River say when told it was going to help make land?
"My sediments exactly."

Where does the Mississippi River go to exercise?
The Riverwalk.

Where is a good place for an apple to work?
At the Core of Engineers.

What do a bandit and river erosion have in common?
They are both bank robbers.

What makes the Breton Sound?
The mouth of the river.

What's the best dessert after eating dirty rice?
Mississippi mud pie.

What beauty queen is hard to spell?
Miss Mississippi.

If the Gulf of Mexico opened a grocery store,
what would it have to have?
A Grand Isle.

What day of the week can't lose weight?
Fat Tuesday.

Why shouldn't you tell someone a secret on Monday?
They might spill the beans.

What do a New Orleans 10K race and jambalaya have in common?
They are both Crescent City Classics.

Where is Easter candy made?
On Elmer's Island.

What kind of suit did the lollipop wear in the summer?
A seersucker.

What tasty treat moves from place to place?
Roman Candy.

What's it like to drive across the Causeway every day?

It takes a toll.

Why did the motorist put on shades?

He was crossing the Sunshine Bridge.

What happened when Lake Pontchartrain got pregnant?

It had Twin Spans.

How did the Huey P. bridge get its name?

It's a Long story.

Whose fault is it that New Orleans has so many potholes?

It's not asphalts.

Why did the cobblestone on the street keep moving around?

It was Toulouse.

How do you build a street in New Orleans?

First you make a rue.

What are some of the holiest places in New Orleans?

The streets of Lakeview.

Where did the primate go for a hike?
Monkey Hill.

What is hard to do at the Audubon Tea Room?
Avoid the elephant in the room.

"Dawlin'?"
"Yes, Ma?"
"Is there a museum that would buy the picture I painted?"
"NO, MA."

What do the New Orleans symphony and the City Park train have in common?
They both have conductors.

Knock knock.
> *Who Dat?*

Audubon.
> *Audubon who?*

You Audubon at the Saints game. They won 42 to 0!

Knock knock.
> *Who Dat?*

Bayou.
> *Bayou who?*

There's a big cockroach bayou.

Knock knock.
    Who Dat?
Earl.
    Earl who?
Can you help me change my Earl?

Knock knock.
    Who Dat?
A two.
    A two who?
A two Fay.

Knock knock.
    Who Dat?
Oyster.
    Oyster who?
Oyster dressing. Please don't open the door!

What is the first thing a Southern baby learns?
How to drawl.

Where's a good place to raise a child in New Orleans?
On Burping Street.

What's another name for baby alligators?
Gator tots.

Why is the St. Louis Cathedral so popular?
It has Mass appeal.

Where does the pope go to relax when he visits
New Orleans?
Pontiff Playground.

What happened when someone stole the chimes
from the church on the West Bank?
There was a Belle Chasse.

What did the man say when John the Baptist
asked him where he wanted to sit?
"By you, St. John."

Where do jeans pop out of the earth?
Denham Springs.

What pirate liked to wear denim?
Jean Lafitte.

Where did Jean Lafitte like to bowl?
In Pirate's Alley.

What Dat?
A Glossary of New Orleans Terms

Algiers (Al-JEERS)—The second-oldest neighborhood in New Orleans, located on the West Bank.

au lait (oh lay)—Prepared with milk, the way many New Orleanians prefer their coffee.

beignet (ben-YAY)—A square piece of dough deep-fried and covered with powdered sugar.

Belle Chasse (Bell Chase)—A small town located in Plaquemines Parish, south of New Orleans.

boudin (BOO-dan)—A Cajun sausage.

Bourré (BOO-ray)—A Cajun card game.

Boutte (Boo-TEE)—A small town located west of New Orleans.

cher (sha)—A term of endearment meaning darling, dear, or sweetheart.

cochon de lait (co-SHON duh lay)—A young pig.

Cut Off—A small town south of New Orleans in Lafourche Parish.

dressed—A sandwich is dressed when it has lettuce, tomato, and mayonnaise.

Elmer's—A famous Louisiana chocolate factory best known for its Gold Brick and Heavenly Hash Easter eggs. It is also a small island off the coast of Louisiana.

étouffée (ay-too-FAY)—From the French word "to smother." A thick stew of crawfish or shrimp cooked with onion, celery, and green bell pepper and served over rice.

Hogs for the Cause—An annual charity pig roast held in New Orleans.

Hubig (HEW-big)—Fruit-filled fried pies made by the Simon Hubig company in New Orleans.

jambalaya (jam-buh-LIE-yuh)—A classic New Orleans dish made of rice, sausage, chicken, seafood, and tomatoes.

Jean Lafitte (Zhon Lah-FEET)—A French pirate who operated in the Gulf of Mexico and helped defeat the British in the Battle of New Orleans.

krewe (crew)—Any New Orleans Mardi Gras group that organizes annual parades.

Leidenheimer (LIE-dun-high-mur) and Reising (RIZE-ing)—Two popular brands of New Orleans French bread.

Lucky Dogs—Hot dogs sold from carts in the French Quarter.

Margaret Orr—A well-known New Orleans meteorologist.

Michoud (MEE-shoo)—A NASA manufacturing facility in New Orleans.

Mr. Bingle—A beloved New Orleans snowman and Santa helper.

muffaletta—A sandwich that originated among New Orleans' Italian immigrants, served on round Sicilian sesame bread and containing layers of salami, ham, cheese, and olive salad.

neutral ground—The New Orleans term for a median.

Papa Noel—What Cajuns call Santa Claus.

Pirate's Alley—The alleyway between St. Louis Cathedral and the Cabildo, where pirates such as Jean Lafitte are said to have met.

pirogue (PEA-rohg)—A small, flat-bottomed boat ideal for paddling through Louisiana bayous.

po' boy—A popular New Orleans sandwich

made of fried shrimp, fried oysters, roast beef, or cold cuts served on French bread.

Pontiff Playground—The oldest public playground in Jefferson Parish, named in memory of LSU baseball standout Wally Pontiff, Jr.

Roman Candy—Taffy sold on the streets of New Orleans from a mule-drawn carriage.

roux (roo)—Flour and fat cooked together. Making a roux is the first step in cooking gumbo, cher.

shotgun—A narrow style of home popular in New Orleans, with rooms arranged one behind the other and doors at the front and back of the house.

shrimp boots—White rubber boots worn by workers on shrimp boats.

turducken—A deboned chicken stuffed into a deboned duck, which is then stuffed into a deboned turkey and roasted or deep-fried.